PREHISTORIC!

THE RISE OF HUMANS

by
David West

A⁺
Smart Apple Media

Published by Smart Apple Media, an imprint of Black Rabbit Books
P.O. Box 3263, Mankato, Minnesota 56002
www.blackrabbitbooks.com

Produced by David West 🧍🧍 Children's Books
6 Princeton Court, 55 Felsham Road, London SW15 1AZ

Designed and illustrated by David West

Library of Congress Cataloging-in-Publication Data

West, David, 1956-
The rise of humans / David West.
    pages cm. -- (Prehistoric!)
Includes index.
ISBN 978-1-62588-087-1 (library binding)
ISBN 978-1-62588-114-4 (paperback)
1. Fossil hominids--Juvenile literature. 2. Human evolution--Juvenile literature. I. Title.
GN282.W47 2015
569.9--dc23

2013036566

Printed in China
CPSIA compliance information: DWCB14CP
010114

9 8 7 6 5 4 3 2 1

Contents

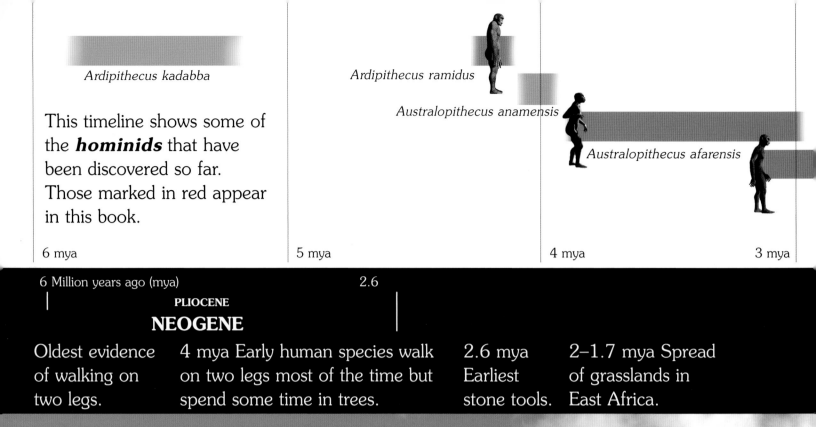

Ardipithecus kadabba

This timeline shows some of the **hominids** that have been discovered so far. Those marked in red appear in this book.

Ardipithecus ramidus

Australopithecus anamensis

Australopithecus afarensis

6 mya   5 mya   4 mya   3 mya

6 Million years ago (mya)   2.6

PLIOCENE
NEOGENE

| Oldest evidence of walking on two legs. | 4 mya Early human species walk on two legs most of the time but spend some time in trees. | 2.6 mya Earliest stone tools. | 2–1.7 mya Spread of grasslands in East Africa. |

Becoming Human

Over a long period of time, early humans adapted to a changing world and evolved into the species we are today. The earliest humans climbed trees and also walked on the ground. As forests disappeared and grasslands took over, our ancestors left the trees and **evolved** into **bipeds**. As they spread, leaving Africa, they evolved body shapes that helped them survive in hot and cold climates. These environmental challenges and larger bodies, led to bigger and more complex brains.

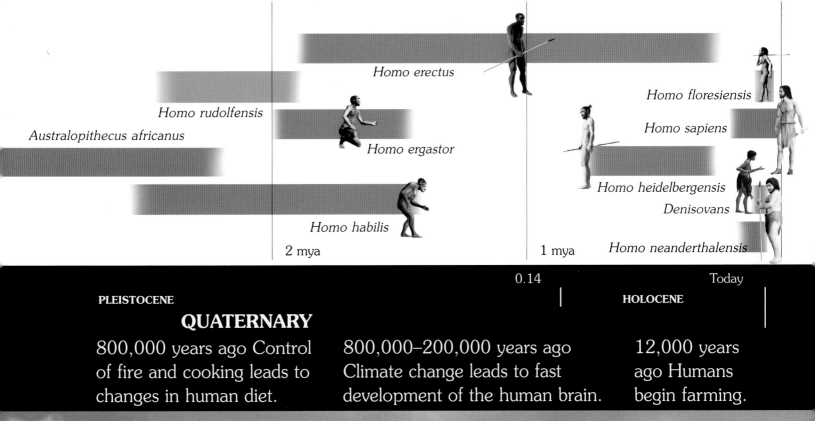

Homo erectus

Homo rudolfensis

Homo floresiensis

Australopithecus africanus

Homo sapiens

Homo ergastor

Homo heidelbergensis

Denisovans

Homo habilis

2 mya

1 mya

Homo neanderthalensis

0.14

Today

PLEISTOCENE

HOLOCENE

QUATERNARY

800,000 years ago Control of fire and cooking leads to changes in human diet.

800,000–200,000 years ago Climate change leads to fast development of the human brain.

12,000 years ago Humans begin farming.

SOCIAL ANIMALS

Early groups of humans began to collect tools and food from various places and take them to favorite eating spots. Sharing with other members of the group led to stronger social bonds, which helped the group's chances of survival. As brain sizes increased, so did the length of time it took for a child to grow up. This meant a safe environment was needed while the young developed. Large groups made caring for the young safer.

A social group of *Homo erectus* was able to survive by evolving to meet the rigors of a changing climate.

Ground Monkeys

Ardipithecus, which means "ground monkey," lived in East Africa around 4.4 million years ago during the Pliocene period. A partial skeleton of a female, known as "Ardi," shows a combination of human and other **primate** traits.

Paleoanthropologists think that *Ardipithecus ramidus* moved in the trees because it had a grasping big toe. They also appeared to have walked on two legs when they moved on the ground.

A pair of *Ardipithecus ramidus* emerge from the trees of a forest in Eastern Africa during the Pliocene epoch.

By examining the skeleton's teeth, scientists think *Ardipithecus ramidus* were probably omnivores, which means they had a diet of plants, meat, and fruit. It seems they did not eat hard, tough foods such as nuts. *Ardipithecus ramidus* lived in a woodland habitat and probably spent a lot of time in the trees to pluck fruits to eat while keeping safe from most **predators**.

Ardipithecus ramidus grew to about 3.9 feet (1.2 m) tall.

3

Lucy

Australopithecus afarensis, meaning "Southern ape of the Afar region," is one of the best-known early human **species**. Remains of more than 3,000 individuals have been found. This includes a female nicknamed "Lucy." This species lived between 3.85 and 2.95 million years ago in Eastern Africa during the Pliocene epoch.

Remains of *Australopithecus afarensis* show the species had both ape and human characteristics. They had apelike faces with a flat nose, a

A family of *Australopithecus afarensis* (1) wander through light woodlands of Eastern Africa during the Pliocene epoch. In the background antelope (2) and elephants (3) graze on the vegetation.

strongly projecting lower jaw, and a small brain that was about one-third the size of a modern human brain. They had long, strong arms and hands ideal for climbing trees. They could walk on two legs, but differently from the way we do. They ate a mainly vegetarian diet, including leaves, fruit, seeds, roots, nuts, and insects, probably with the occasional small lizard.

Australopithecus afarensis grew to about 3.7 feet (1.1 m) tall.

African Southern Ape

Australopithecus africanus, meaning "African Southern Ape," lived in Southern Africa about 3.3 to 2.1 million years ago during the Pliocene and early Pleistocene epochs. They looked similar to *Australopithecus afarensis* with human and apelike features.

Australopithecus africanus had a rounder skull containing a larger brain. The skeletons suggest they walked on two legs, but they were also able to swing from the branches of trees.

A group of *Australopithecus africanus* walk from the safety of a tree across a valley in Southern Africa during the late Pliocene. They keep a wary eye out for lions and other predators that hunt them.

They had a diet similar to modern chimpanzees, which consisted of fruit, plants, nuts, seeds, roots, insects, and eggs. Scientists have found animal bones alongside the remains of those of *Australopithecus africanus*. At first, they thought this species must have hunted these animals. Later, it was thought that predators such as lions and leopards were responsible.

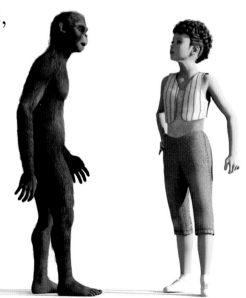

Australopithecus africanus grew up to 4.5 feet (1.4 m) tall.

1

Handyman

Homo habilis lived in Africa approximately 2.4 to 1.4 million years ago. They had a short body and long, ape-like arms similar to the australopithecines. But they differed from the earlier hominids in that they had a large brain and small teeth.

Scientists think *Homo habilis* might be the ancestor of *Homo ergaster* (see pages 14–15), which in turn gave rise to *Homo erectus*. *Homo habilis*, which means "skilled man," was given this name because they

In a scene from early pleistocene Africa, a group of *Homo habilis* (1) have found a dead *Deinotherium* (2) and are in the process of butchering it.

were thought to be the first stone toolmakers. The oldest stone tools, however, are dated slightly earlier. Forest foods such as fruit became scarce during this time. It forced *Homo habilis* to seek new sources such as meat by scavenging on dead animals. Stone tools were used to cut meat from carcasses and smash open animal bones to extract the **nutritious** marrow.

Homo habilis was about 4.3 feet (1.3 m) tall.

2

Working Man

Homo ergaster, meaning "working man" due to the many tools the species made, lived from 1.8 to 1.3 million years ago. Some scientists consider them to be the African version of *Homo erectus* (see pages 16–17).

An almost complete skeleton of *Homo ergaster* was found in West Turkana in Kenya, Africa, and was named "Turkana Boy." About 8 to 10 years of age when he died, he was already 5.2 feet (1.6 m) tall and may have reached 6.1 feet (1.86 m) as an adult.

In this scene from Pleistocene Africa, a *Homo ergaster* (1) is about to butcher a small buck with a hand axe. His companion shouts out a warning as a *Dinofelis* (2) suddenly appears and is intent on stealing his food.

His anatomy has given scientists a good idea of what *Homo ergaster* may have looked like. Their tall, slender bodies were ideal for walking across the large **savannah** plains. They also had a more human-like face. Their noses projected outward. Their braincase was more domed to allow for a larger brain.

Homo ergaster could grow to over 6 feet (1.8 m) tall.

Out of Africa

Homo erectus, meaning "upright man," lived from about 1.8 million years ago to about 143,000 years ago. The species originated in Africa and spread as far as Europe, Georgia, India, Sri Lanka, China, and Java. It is generally considered to have been the first hominid species to have traveled beyond Africa.

Homo erectus are the oldest known early humans to have possessed the modern human body proportions with long legs and shorter arms.

A small hunter-gatherer group of *Homo erectus* (1) walk through grasslands filled with game and a pair of *Elasmotheriums* (2) as they travel from Africa into Asia. One of their members returns from a successful hunting trip.

They were possibly the first humans to live in small, **hunter-gatherer** groups and may have used rafts to travel the oceans. Evidence shows *Homo erectus* used fire and may have been able to make fire. Despite their human-like anatomy, they may not have been capable of producing modern human speech. More likely, they used simple speaking sounds to communicate with each other.

Homo erectus grew up to 6.1 feet (1.9 m) tall .

17

1

Hunters

Homo heidelbergensis lived about 700,000 to 200,000 years ago in Europe, Africa, and possibly Asia. They are named after the place they were first found near Heidelberg, Germany. They were a close relative and probably a descendant of *Homo ergaster.*

Homo heidelbergensis were first to hunt large animals regularly. Many spears have been found that are weighted at the ends to be thrown like javelins. They lived alongside horses, *megaloceros* (giant deer),

A group of *Homo heidelbergensis* (1) attack a cave bear (2) with spears in a scene from Pleistocene Europe.

elephants, rhinoceros, and wolves. They were first to build shelters made out of wood and rock. Evidence of fireplaces suggests they could make and control fire. Scientists think that *Homo heidelbergensis* may have made spears and tools for social display as well as hunting. This suggests ritual behavior and, perhaps, that these early humans were developing complex minds.

Homo heidelbergensis grew to 5.8 feet (1.8 m) tall.

1

Neanderthals

Neanderthals lived between 200,000 and 28,000 years ago during the Pleistocene epoch in Europe and parts of western and central Asia. The species is named after Neander's Valley in Germany where it was first discovered.

Neanderthals looked similar to modern humans only shorter, more heavily built, and much stronger—especially in the arms. **Fossils** of their skulls show that they had no chin and backward sloping

20

A mammoth (1) has wandered into a narrow gully following the scent of fresh water, but it has walked into a trap. A group of *Homo neanderthalensis*, more commonly known as Neanderthals (2), rush out to throw spears. Others hurl rocks from the cliffs above.

foreheads. Living in cold climates, they had a pronounced brow ridge and a large nose to warm the air they breathed in. Evidence of injuries suggests that hunting involved close contact with large animals such as mammoths. Neanderthals ate a lot of meat, but also supplemented their diet with vegetables and fruit. They made simple clothes from animal skins. Evidence shows that they buried their dead.

Homo neanderthalensis was about 5.5 feet (1.7 m) tall.

1

Denisova Girl

In 2008, hominid bones were discovered in the remote Denisova cave in the Altai Mountains of Siberia. These belong to a group of early humans that lived at the same time as Neanderthals and early *Homo sapiens*.

Little is known of the features of Denisovans since very few skeletal remains have been found. A finger and toe bone, along with teeth, are all that have been discovered. It seems they were very similar to *Homo erectus*. They may have descended from these early humans who were

A young Denisova girl (1) hides with her catch as a group of Neanderthals (2) pass by in this scene from the late Pleistocene of Eurasia.

the first to leave Africa (see pages 16–17) or the ancient human *Homo heidelbergensis* who lived about 500,000 years ago. Evidence shows that Denisovans **interbred** with early *Homo sapiens*. **Genetic** evidence shows that Denisova **ancestry** is shared by Melanesians, Australian Aborigines, and small groups of people in Southeast Asia.

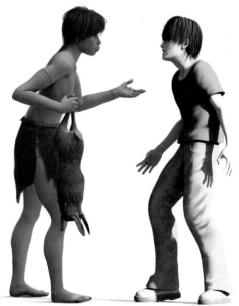

Denisova girl was a child with brown hair, skin, and eyes.

23

Little People

Discovered in 2003 on the island of Flores in Indonesia, *Homo floresiensis* lived between 95,000 to 17,000 years ago. Due to their small stature and big feet, they have been nicknamed "hobbit" after the small people of Middle-earth in J. R. R. Tolkien's fiction story.

As well as having a small body size, *Homo floresiensis* had a remarkably small brain. Despite this, it was still an intelligent hominid. A cave where their remains were found shows evidence of cooking with fire.

In this scene from late Pleistocene Indonesia, a family of *Homo floresiensis* (1) gather around a dead *Stegodon* calf (2), which they will cut up and cook in their cave.

Stegodon bones associated with the hominids show cut marks. Other stone tools show that these little hominids hunted large elephant-like animals called *Stegodons*. They also shared the island with giant rats and Komodo dragons. Scientists think *Homo floresiensis* evolved from *Homo erectus*. After *Homo erectus* moved to Flores, it began to shrink in size over the generations by a process known as **island dwarfism**.

Homo floresiensis grew to 3.5 feet (1.1 m) tall.

1

Cro-Magnon

Cro-Magnon, also known as European Early Modern Humans, is the name used to describe the first early modern humans (*Homo sapiens*) of the European late Pleistocene. They are named after a rock shelter in France called Cro-Magnon.

The Cro-Magnons shared the European landscape with Neanderthals for 10,000 years or more before the Neanderthals became **extinct**. These hunter-gatherers were tall and differed from modern humans by

26

A group of Cro-Magnons (1) bury their dead (2) in a religious ceremony at night in this scene from 33,000 years ago in Western Europe.

their thick-set **physique**. They had fairly low skulls, wide faces, prominent noses, and a strong jaw. Cro-Magnon could probably speak. Big-game hunters, they killed mammoths, cave bears, horses, and reindeer using throwing spears with flint heads. Their diet included fruit and vegetables as well as meat.

Cro-Magnon grew to 5.9 feet (1.8 m) tall.

Wise Men

Homo sapiens, meaning wise man, evolved in Africa about 200,000 years ago. They spread throughout the world and are what scientists call modern humans. They are the only human species living today.

Anatomically, modern humans have lighter skeletons compared with earlier humans. The skull is a thin-walled, high skull with a flat and nearly vertical forehead. Modern human faces do not have the heavy

28

A cave in Europe is home to a group of *Homo sapiens* gathering by a fire where meat is cooking. One member is painting on the cave wall (1). Females with heavy brows (2) show evidence of earlier interbreeding with *Homo neanderthalensis* (see pages 20–21).

brow ridges of other early humans. The jaws are also less heavy with smaller teeth. Prehistoric *Homo sapiens* specialized in stone tools and made a variety of refined and specialized tools. These include fishhooks, harpoons, bows and arrows, spear throwers, and sewing needles. As they became more sophisticated, they practiced rituals and ceremonies, which involved painting animals on cave walls.

Homo sapiens grew up to 6 feet (1.8 m) tall.

Fact File

Ardipithecus ramidus
"Ground monkey"
nickname: Ardi
3.9 feet (1.2 m) tall
Eastern Africa
4.4 mya
(pp. 6–7)

Australopithecus afarensis
"Southern ape of the Afar region"
nickname: Lucy
Males: 4.9 feet (1.5 m) tall
Females: 3.5 feet (1 m) tall
Eastern Africa
3.85 to 2.95 mya
(pp. 8–9)

Australopithecus africanus
"African Southern Ape"
nickname: Taung Child
Males: 4.5 feet (1.4 m) tall
Females: 3.7 feet (1.1 m) tall
Southern Africa
3.3 to 2.1 mya
(pp. 10–11)

Homo habilis
"Skilled man"
nickname: Handy Man
3.3–4.5 feet (1–1.4 m) tall
Eastern and Southern Africa
2.4 to 1.4 mya
(pp. 12–13)

Homo ergaster
"Working man"
nickname: Turkana Boy
3.3–4.5 feet (1–1.4 m) tall
Eastern and Southern Africa
1.8 to 1.3 mya
(pp. 14–15)

Homo erectus
"Upright man"
nickname: Java Man and Peking Man
4.7–6.1 feet (1.4–1.9 m) tall
Northern, Eastern, and Southern Africa; Western Asia, East Asia
1.8 mya to 143,000 years ago
(pp. 16–17)

Homo heidelbergensis
"Man from Heidelberg"
nickname: Rhodesian Man
Males: 5.7 feet (1.7 m) tall
Females: 5.2 feet (1.6 m) tall
Europe, possibly Asia, Eastern and Southern Africa
700,000 to 200,000 years ago
(pp. 18–19)

Homo neanderthalensis
"Man from Neanderthal"
nickname: Neanderthal
Males: 5.5 feet (1.7 m) tall
Females: 5.2 feet (1.6 m) tall
Europe and southwestern to central Asia
200,000 to 28,000 years ago
(pp. 20–21)

Denisova hominin
Species of *Homo*
nickname: X-woman
size unknown
Europe, possibly Asia, Eastern and Southern Africa
50,000 to 30,000 years ago
(pp. 22–23)

Homo floresiensis
"Man from Flores"
nickname: Hobbit
Females: 3.5 feet (1.1 m) tall
Indonesia
95,000 to 17,000 years ago
(pp. 24–25)

European early modern human (*Homo sapiens*)
nickname: Cro-Magnon
5.9 feet (1.8 m) tall
Europe
43,000 to 20,000 years ago
(pp. 26–27)

Homo sapiens
"Wise man"
nickname: Modern man
6 feet (1.8 m) tall
Worldwide
200,000 years ago to today
(pp. 28–29)

Glossary

ancestry The evolutionary line of descent of an animal or plant.

biped An animal that uses only two legs for walking.

evolve To develop gradually from a simple to a more complex form.

extinct When a species or group of living things dies out and no longer exists.

fossils The remains of living things that have turned to rock.

genetic Relating to the origin of an animal's or plant's characteristics.

Holocene Geological epoch which began 11,700 years ago and continues to today.

hominid A member of the family of Hominidae that includes humans and their fossil ancestors.

hunter-gatherer A member of a type of human species whose food is obtained by hunting and foraging rather than by farming.

interbreed To produce offspring with a member of a different race or species.

island dwarfism The process of the reduction in size of large animals, over a period of time, when the population is limited to a very small environment, usually islands.

Neogene The geological period starting 23 million years ago and ending 2.5 million years ago.

nutritious Providing a high level of nourishment.

paleoanthropologist A scientist who studies humankind and specializes in looking at the fossils of hominids.

physique The size and shape of a person's body.

Pleistocene The geological epoch that lasted from about 2.5 million years ago to 11,700 years ago.

Pliocene The second and youngest epoch of the Neogene Period that extends from 5.3 million to 2.5 million years ago.

predator An animal that hunts other animals for food.

primate Any mammal of the group that includes lemurs, lorises, tarsiers, monkeys, apes, and humans that first appeared during the late Paleocene.

Quaternary The geological period that follows the Neogene Period and spans from 2.5 million years ago to today.

savannah A grassy plain in tropical and subtropical regions, with few trees.

species A group of living organisms consisting of similar individuals capable of interbreeding.

Index